REYNARD

The Story of a Fox
Returned to the Wild

REYNARD

The Story of a Fox
Returned to the Wild

STORY AND PHOTOS BY
ALICE MILLS LEIGHNER

To: Emmy & Tyler
with best wishes and the
hope you enjoy learning about
foxes.
　　　　Alice Mills Leighner
　　　　February 5, 2010

ATHENEUM   1986   NEW YORK

Library of Congress Cataloging-in-Publication Data

Leighner, Alice Mills.
Reynard: the story of a fox returned to the wild.

Includes index.
SUMMARY: Describes the habits and rehabilitation of
a young red fox found on the highway and brought to a
special center, where it was taught how to survive
in the wild before being released again.
1. Red fox — Juvenile literature. 2. Wildlife rescue
—Juvenile literature. [1. Red Fox. 2. Foxes.
3. Wildlife rescue] I. Title.
QL737.C22L48   1986   599.74'442   85-26848
ISBN 0-689-31189-3

Published simultaneously in Canada by
Collier Macmillan Canada Inc.
Composition by Boro Typographers, New York City
Printed and bound by Maple-Vail, Binghamton, New York
Designed by Suzanne Haldane
First edition

To my father,
who has been helping turtles cross the road
for more than sixty years and still does,
and to Michael

REYNARD

The Story of a Fox
Returned to the Wild

This is a story about the adventures of Reynard, a young red fox, and his unusual upbringing. Like other red foxes, Reynard was probably one of four or five fox pups born to his mother in early March. His parents had most likely made a home in an abandoned woodchuck den, enlarging it to meet their family needs. The baby foxes were tiny and covered with brown fuzz. Their eyes were closed for the first ten days.

At night, Reynard's mother and father hunted. The mother would return to the den early in the morning to nurse her young. Later, when they could eat solid food, she brought them mice, small rabbits and, sometimes, insects.

As curious pups, Reynard and his brothers and sisters ventured outside the den when they were about a month old. They played and wrestled with one another and tried to catch insects. They chased each other's tails and sometimes their own. Their father, a handsome dog fox, kept a watchful eye for danger. The young red foxes explored their expanding world while they awaited their mother's return with the "catch of the day."

One night, Reynard became too adventuresome and wandered too far from his den home. Enthusiastically, he explored what seemed to be a very large and interesting world.

Suddenly, he found himself beside a wide, shiny, open black field. It had no protective high grass like the farm fields that red foxes are fond of. It had no camouflaging small trees like those in the light forests where red foxes are found.

This black, shiny, open field was—although Reynard didn't know it—the New York State Thruway and it was a very dangerous place for a little red fox. The fast-moving cars were a hazard to all wild animals.

It began to rain. Reynard was confused and
lost and very frightened.

Reynard, however, was more fortunate than
many other baby animals who find themselves
in similar situations.

Reynard's adventure with humans began near a toll booth on the New York State Thruway. Found shivering with cold and fear by the side of the busy road one rainy April night, Reynard was befriended by a passing motorist who thought he was an abandoned puppy.

The little red fox, who was only about six weeks old, was handed over to a very surprised toll collector. He, in turn, called the Yonkers Animal Shelter.

Animal shelter people usually care for lost or abandoned dogs and cats. Workers at the shelters try to either reunite these pets with their families or to find them good homes. Mrs. Schliman at the shelter immediately saw that Reynard was a red fox, not a bedraggled puppy.

She gently dried him with a portable hair dryer and fed him a big bowl of puppy food.

Since animal shelters are better equipped to care for domesticated pets, such as cats and dogs, Mrs. Schliman contacted an organization called Wildcare.

Wildcare is made up of volunteers in Westchester County, New York, who raise and take care of abandoned or injured wild animals. They have helped baby deer, opposums, raccoons, skunks, woodchucks, squirrels, rabbits, birds, and—of course—foxes.

When these baby animals are old enough to be able to survive in nature, they are released to live as their parents and grandparents before them—wild and free.

Reynard was introduced to a meeting of Wildcare volunteers. Even though he was still very small he was able to scamper around quickly, for foxes are noted for their speed. A fox at a dead run has been estimated to reach speeds around forty-five miles an hour. Some naturalists think they can run much faster.

Like all red foxes, Reynard had a tiny white tip at the end of his tail.

Dona Lakin became Reynard's "mother." She wore heavy leather gloves when first handling Reynard, until she was sure the little red fox didn't bite.

It was Dona who gave him the name Reynard. "Reynard" is old French for "red fox."

Like all young red fox pups, Reynard was covered with soft, woolly brown fur. His face was somewhat blunt—not nearly as pointed as it would be later as he became an adult fox. Reynard's paws were black—as were the backs of his huge pointed ears.

Photo by Glen Tracy

Most of Wildcare's babies come in whole
litters of raccoons, opposums, rabbits and
skunks. They play with and learn from each
other. Reynard had only Dona for company, and
she spent a lot of time with him so he wouldn't
be lonesome.

Theirs was a very special relationship. Sometimes Dona just held Reynard and told him that he was the most beautiful red fox in the whole world.

Then Reynard might give Dona a big kiss.

Dona often took Reynard to a nature sanctuary that had a huge outdoor cage. Here he could run and play with sticks and develop the speed and agility that are the trademark of the red fox. Sometimes, Reynard just sat looking at the big outside world.

At home, in the kitchen, Reynard begged Dona to pick him up and hold him. He wanted lots of attention.

While Reynard was as friendly with Dona as a puppy would be with his new family, he remained very cautious with people he didn't know. This pleased Dona, for it would be dangerous if Reynard became too tame and trusting of all humans.

Dona was happy when Reynard showed wild fox instincts. Man and his machines (like the car) are about the only enemies of the clever fox. In most areas where the fox lives there are none of his natural enemies left—wolves and lynx and bobcats.

Some of America's red foxes, which are closely related to dogs, are descendants of native foxes. Others are descended from the eight pairs of red foxes brought here from England in 1650. These were turned loose in Maryland so that rich colonists could have fox hunts.

Fox hunting is a sport in which men and women dress in fancy riding clothes, mount fast horses and, with a pack of yipping dogs, chase the fox through the countryside.

Wildcare and other animal rehabilitation organizations have as their goal to raise babies such as Reynard so that they are healthy but

not too dependent on humans. Each Wildcare
parent teaches his or her adopted baby animals
the skills they will need to survive in their
natural habitat. These volunteers work to
develop natural instincts just as the animal's
own mother would. Volunteers temper their
natural affection so as not to make pets of the
wild babies.

Sometimes it is hard not to become too
attached to these little furry orphans. When an
animal is as friendly as Reynard, with such a
sweet personality, it is difficult not to worry
about their well-being once they are free.

But, just as with mothers of human children,
there comes a time when it is right for the
young adult to go it alone.

Reynard loved to pounce on feet and pretend he was attacking prey. In this way, he developed swiftness and cunning.

He often made surprise attacks, catching Dona off guard. The slightest wiggle of a human toe would cause Reynard to spring into action.

Dona found this game a bit painful, but Reynard was busy practicing fox skills.

Another favorite learning game for Reynard was playing with small objects, much as a kitten or puppy does. He especially liked film cans. These film containers were small and round and rolled easily.

Reynard never tired of pouncing on the small black cans. He loved to hit them with his elegant black paws and toss them high in the air. He shook them and tossed them and batted them.

These were skills Reynard would later use with frozen mice and eventually with live mice.

People who saw Reynard always commented on the size of his ears and teeth.

A fox has large, erect ears and a very keen sense of hearing. He can hear the smallest sound that might signal approaching danger. Even more importantly, a fox can hear the faint sound of a mouse or small rabbit moving in the underbrush. Hearing is one of the red fox's most important senses for helping him locate his next meal.

Oval eyes with vertical pupils are also characteristic of the red fox. Their eyes are like those of a cat: a dog has round eyes. Foxes are nocturnal and hunt their food between dusk and dawn, and, like cats, they are thought to have good nighttime vision.

However, like a dog, Reynard has forty-two teeth. Foxes have and lose their baby teeth just like puppies and young children do.

But foxes do not chew their food like people. They gulp it whole. If a piece of meat is too large to be eaten whole, the fox uses his power-ful jaws and long, sharp "carnassial" teeth like scissors to tear off a piece of meat small enough to be swallowed.

"Yippee! Paper towels," Reynard seems to be saying. He had quickly learned that when Dona got out the paper towels, it meant that she was preparing to dry a thawed mouse for him.

Dona kept a whole freezer full of frozen mice. She didn't even have room for ice cube trays or packages of frozen vegetables or ice cream because the mice took up all the space.

Reynard wasn't the only Wildcare orphan who ate mice—Dona also had an injured Great Horned Owl and a Red-tailed Hawk who ate their share of mice with the same enthusiasm.

Reynard would stand on his hind paws to beg for his mouse. Even in nature, red foxes sometimes stand up when they are looking and listening for danger or for a potential source of food.

Mice and other small rodents make up a large portion of a fox's diet. They also like insects, grapes, other fruits and corn-on-the-cob.

After Dona gave Reynard his mouse, he galloped around the kitchen, shaking it to "kill" it. Wild foxes break their prey's necks and play with their food much as cats and some dogs do.

Reynard would later find a quiet spot under the kitchen table and crunch the mouse—bones and all. He would sometimes turn his head sideways, efficiently using his carnassial teeth to scissor the mouse in half.

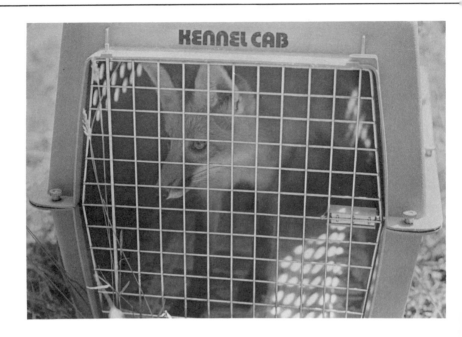

By mid-June, Reynard's kennel cab was too small to take him to the outdoor exercise cage.

Wildcare volunteers Glen and Jeff were busy building him a huge habitat pen that would provide Reynard with shelter from wind and rain.

In it, there were small trees like those in the open forest that red foxes like. There were rock ledges for Reynard to climb.

Dona put Reynard's carrier case in the huge habitat cage, which was near Jeff's cabin in the woods. She opened the door and Reynard stepped out into a new and exciting world that more nearly resembled the home his parents had provided so long ago.

Sometimes, Reynard would go to the front opening of his cave and look out at his expanding world.

Unlike gray foxes, red foxes do not live in dens year round. Even in winter, red foxes sleep outside with their great bushy tails covering their paws and noses to protect these sensitive body parts from cold and wind. Mother foxes use a den only in spring when they are raising their babies.

Still, Reynard seemed to like his den as it provided shelter while he became used to living outdoors again. The rock cave also gave Reynard a place to hide from the eyes of visiting people.

Sometimes, Reynard climbed the rock ledges and stood in the sunlight looking very alert and foxy. He always seemed to be smiling.

At other times, Reynard crouched at the cave's entrance—his ears pricked forward to listen intently, ready to pounce on and attack any real or imagined prey.

Since he had been living outdoors in the habitat cage, Reynard's tail had become gloriously full.

Foxes use their tails for balance when turning and maneuvering. With the help of this tail, a red fox can turn "on a dime" to elude danger.

When Dona came to visit Reynard a month later, he was very excited. He climbed high on his rock ledge and kissed Dona's eyes.

Dona was pleased that Reynard still considered her "mom."

Dona brought a frozen mouse for Reynard. This was a wonderful treat after the usual meals of dog food. Jeff had been unsuccessful in trapping field mice in his cabin. Because it was summer, the mice had all moved outside—or perhaps they had smelled Reynard and left for safer territory.

Dona promised Reynard an even better surprise, which she would bring on her next visit—a female fox (called a vixen).

"Foxy" was the little vixen's name. Although she was about the same age as Reynard, she was only half his size. Foxy had lovely black-tipped ears.

She had been the victim of one of the most dangerous enemies of today's modern fox—a fast moving automobile.

A favorite patient at the Cross River Animal Hospital, Foxy had free run of the x-ray room.

Sometimes Foxy checked out the cats in the cages. She enjoyed human attention as well and was very friendly to people.

Like all red foxes, Foxy has a black spot near the base of her tail. This marks a scent gland. Adult red foxes have a distinct smell—something like the musky odor of a skunk. This smell, sometimes called the "reek of the fox" helps foxes identify and communicate with one another.

Dona arrived one day carrying the portable cage. Reynard seemed excited. He put his front paws on a big rock and gave Dona and Foxy his most endearing smile.

But he flattened his ears and cautiously approached Foxy when she was put in the cage, sniffing her with his sensitive nose.

Then, approaching Foxy from a large rock above, Reynard wagged his tail. Foxy laid back her ears and made nasty clicking noises with her teeth. Reynard backed off.

Each time Reynard approached Foxy the same thing happened. Finally, Reynard went off alone to his rock den. The two foxes didn't actually fight but they weren't the best of friends either. They simply tolerated one another.

By early September, Reynard and Foxy had acquired the swiftness and skill to catch live mice. At first, when Jeff put live mice in the cage the foxes were only curious. But quickly instincts surfaced and in no time they learned how to catch their evening meal.

Occasionally, when Foxy's and Reynard's hunger was satisfied, they would take leftover small nuggets of dog food—or sometimes a dead mouse—and cache them away for later.

Foxes, when food is plentiful, often dig small holes. Then they bury their food and carefully cover it with dirt.

These caches of leftover food served Reynard and Foxy later when they were hungry. This form of fox behavior is similar to the pattern of squirrels who bury nuts against a day when food may be in short supply.

The red foxes were becoming more aloof
even toward the humans they knew. They grew
restless. These were signs that Reynard and
Foxy were ready for freedom.

Jeff had planned to cut the mesh on the
habitat cage on a cool and cloudy day in
September. But Reynard had already decided
that that day was the right one for freedom.
He had taken a running leap at the fence and
escaped before dawn. Reynard's self-release
confirmed Dona's and Jeff's decision that the
red foxes were ready and eager to become wild
and free.

Foxy watched the opening of the gate with curiosity and some apprehension. She retreated to the safety of the familiar rock cave. Jeff tried to coax her out—to no avail.

Foxy circled the pen several times, showing no apparent interest in the open door. She climbed up on the great rock, wrapped her elegant tail around her paws and fell asleep. Dona and Jeff just had to wait.

An hour passed. Then another half-hour.
Dusk approached. Foxy awoke rested and finally
ready to investigate the open door. Cautiously
she approached the opening.

Stepping carefully through the opening, Foxy hugged the outside of the fence. Then she bounded through the brush to join Reynard somewhere in the light forests and open fields that have been the terrain of the American red fox for centuries.